STRAIGHT ROWS

Life's Success Lessons Learned From Being Raised On A Farm.

Short stories about life's lessons learned
on the farm and how those lessons
can be learned in a city environment.

By
Max Harris

Dedicated to my parents
Arlyss and Melva Harris

PREFACE

My first eighteen years were spent on a south central Kansas wheat and dairy farm thirteen miles from the nearest town and one mile from our nearest neighbors. My brother, five years older, and I were the only children in the family. Our father was the fourth generation of our family to farm in the area. Our mother was from a northern Nebraska farm and had ventured out to attend a Methodist College in southern Kansas. Her teaching career lead her to the one room rural school where she met the older brother of two of her students. The older brother was to become her husband and our father. My brother was born in 1942 and I was born in 1947.

The family farm and community that were our training grounds are rapidly becoming a thing of the past. Most farm children left the farm during the past generation due to the advent of new technology, larger equipment and larger farms. There was simply no room for them to return to the farm. Members of this "Exodus Generation" carry experiences and knowledge that few in our country will ever have again. At the time I thought some of the experiences weren't all that pleasant, but as I've grown older I've come to appreciate the long-term benefits they had on my life. As a member of the "Exodus Generation" I felt it would be significant to put those experiences and lessons to print for present and future generations to see.

My brother and I both left the farm, chose different occupations and found significant success in our chosen fields. What were the lessons we learned that served us so well? Hopefully this book will bring some of them to light.

I was fortunate that my first job after college brought me to a young entrepreneurial advertising executive that was interested in helping his employees grow. He sent us to a class based on the book "Psycho-Cybernetics" by Maxwell Maltz. The book, based on "self-image" and the importance of setting goals for yourself, tweaked my curiosity and lead me to many more self-help type books. I found these books to be very interesting. As I was reading them, I always had the feeling that somehow I already knew what they were saying. It wasn't until I chose to slow down my career that I had the time to analyze those feelings and realize that most of the self-help book lessons had already been learned by me through my experience of being raised on a farm.

As many great thinkers have demonstrated, ideas and lessons are easier to understand and remember when they are portrayed through a short story. When I looked back on my formative years I discovered that many of the key lessons I learned were in fact part of a short story. I chose, then, to use the short story format to present my thoughts. Hopefully you will find the stories to be both helpful and interesting.

CONTENTS

Preface   xi

1. Straight Rows   1
2. New Potatoes   8
3. Save for the Future   12
4. A Glass of Milk   17
5. Terraces   22
6. Efficiency Expert   26
7. Time to Dream   31
8. Growing Plants   34
9. The Accident   39
10. The Cemetery   46
11. Helping Others   51
12. Family Meals   57
13. Getting Along With Others   60
14. Take Time for Fun   63
15. Work Ethic   66
16. Public Speaking   72
17. Investments   78
18. Competition   82
19. Honesty   90
20. Conclusion   95

"Your built-in success mechanism must have a goal or target." Maxwell Maltz, "Psycho-Cybernetics"

"To plant a straight row pick a point at the end of the field, keep your eyes on it, and drive directly to it." My farm experience.

1. STRAIGHT ROWS

It was the summer of 1961 and the wheat harvest was in full swing on our south central Kansas farm. I was a 13 year old boy enjoying the excitement. Even though the days were long and the work was hard and dirty it was a fun time because my family and my uncle's family were all working together to complete the job. Farm work can be lonely work, but harvest was different. Everyone pitched in to help. My retired grandfather was there to help wherever he could. Extra hands were hired to help. My cousins and I had jobs to do and it was one of the few times we were able to work together. The women brought meals to the fields so the harvest could continue without breaking for lunch. Work days began at 5:30 A.M. and could last until midnight. We were all participating in a giant race to beat the arrival of harvest threatening weather that might arrive. One hail storm could wipe out the wheat crop and a good deal of our family's income for the year. Wheat harvest time is the end of a 12 month cycle of preparing the soil, planting the seeds, watching the crop grow and reaping the ultimate payout. In a sense it's a time of celebration after 12 months of working and waiting. For me, however, things were about to change.

Early one morning my father announced at the breakfast table that conditions were right for planting the milo crop and it was important that the planting be done now. He looked at me and said he thought I could handle it and was going to start me on it that day. To the casual observer this might not seem like a significant event but to me it was devastating. Number one, it meant that I was going to be separated from the excitement of the harvest. Number two, it meant that I was going to be solely responsible for planting a crop that required precision driving. You see milo is a row crop which means it's planted in wide spaced rows so it can be cultivated at a later date to remove the weeds. This means the rows have to be planted straight so they can be easily cultivated without uprooting the milo crop. But I was well aware there was more to the necessity of straight rows than the practical side. The fact was that in the eyes of my parents, my grandfather and my extended family, the quality of the rows was a direct reflection of your character and in essence the character of the entire family. And there was no way to hide the rows. They would be there for everyone to see every day for the next five months.

Since I was a small child I had heard my father's observations about   straight rows as we drove through the countryside. His ultimate test for a straight row was that you should be able to shoot a rifle down the row without hitting a plant. While I understood the importance of straight rows it never really occurred to me that some day I would be entrusted with the responsibility. But the time had come and I was about to receive a lesson that in reality had more to do with the proper way of thinking than it did with the mechanics of driving a tractor. It was a way of thinking that was to serve me well for the rest of my life.

I was nervous when we finally reached the field with the planter.   Nothing had been said but I believe he sensed my concern and before we began to plant he said, "Well, here's the way you plant straight rows." His message went something like this;

"First, pick a point at the end of the field where you want the row to end.   In this case it was a pole with a white flag attached that my father had placed there earlier to mark boundaries of the field.

Next, sit in the tractor seat and visually center the radiator cap of the tractor on the line of sight to the pole.

Make sure you have the planter in the ground correctly.

Drive directly to the pole.

Pay attention to what you're doing.

Don't take your eyes off the pole.

Keep the radiator cap centered on the pole.

Keep the steering wheel steady.

Don't be looking back to admire how you're doing or you'll end up with crooked rows .

If you have to stop be sure you have the pole lined up on the radiator cap again before you start."

He made the first round for me and set the standards for the field. I noticed how he kept a steady hand on the wheel and a constant gaze at the distant pole. Looking back now, I'm sure he was doing the best he could do to impress the importance of the task to his son. After he completed the first round of the field I was informed that there was still more to learn.

He stopped the tractor and looked me straight in

the eyes with a look that fathers reserve for sons when they want to make sure they're paying attention. I've used the look myself a few times. He said something like this;

"Just because you've got one straight row, it doesn't mean you can start goofing off. You've got to keep working at it every round."

He explained that I couldn't sight the tractor on the pole anymore because it would be too far to the side. That's why the planter had an arm that left a guide line in the dirt to follow. By centering the tractor on the guide line and keeping it there I would continue to plant straight rows. "However," he said, "it's almost impossible to plant a perfect row so each time you start a new round look down the entire distance of the guide line and drive to correct any bends that may have developed.

If you just keep following a mistake it will get worse and worse with each round.

Keep making corrections with each round.

Pay attention to what you're doing."

Then he left, knowing that I would do a good job, and I did. What I don't believe he knew was that he was teaching me a way of thinking that would help guide me successfully through the rest of my life.

I missed the fun of harvest that year, but I discovered a new kind of joy, one that lasted much longer. Each day as I passed by the straight rows I had planted I felt a wonderful feeling of accomplishment. I had been complimented by my father and grandfather about what a fine job I had done. I was sure that other people in the community were also seeing the rows and no doubt were talking about how straight they were. It was a gratification that I was discovering to be just as important as a few days of fun during harvest. It was one that I could enjoy all summer as the milo grew to maturity.

The lessons I learned from this simple farm experience have filled hundreds of pages of self-improvement books with subjects such as;

Setting goals and moving toward them.

Keeping focused on your goals.

Making adjustments when mistakes are inevitably made.

Understanding that your actions have long-term consequences.

Individual responsibility.

Taking pride in your work.

Looking forward not backward.

Delaying gratification.

Following advice from those who know more.

Enjoying accomplishments.

Long-term thinking.

While this one experience obviously made a strong impression on me, farm life was full of many learning experiences. It's a way of life that inherently teaches children many of the lessons they will need to live successful lives. What those lessons were, how they were learned, and ideas on how they can be recreated in a city environment are the objectives of this book.

Our own children, who we raised in the city, are grown, responsible adults and I take great joy in the success they are experiencing. This book is for them, their future children, their children's children and anyone else who is interested in what it means to be "Raised on a Farm."

"The ability to mentally visualize a desired future and take the necessary actions to reach that future is the first step toward achieving any kind of success." My city thoughts.

"If you want new potatoes, you've got to hoe the rows." My farm experience.

2. NEW POTATOES

One of the delights of being raised on a farm was the wonderful food my mother prepared. My favorite was new potatoes. Mother prepared a sauce of unknown origins to me, but I'm sure it must have been a combination of whole milk, cream, butter, salt and pepper. A recipe that would make a cardiovascular doctor faint I'm sure. But the sauce combined with the tender new potatoes was a delicious eating experience I can vividly remember to this day. I remember as a young child asking my mother, "When will the new potatoes be ready to dig?" enough times that she would finally go check to see if they were ready. That involved selecting one of the more mature potato plants from our garden and inserting a four pronged spade into the soil to uproot the plant. I would be on my knees beside her waiting for the clods of soil to fall from the roots to expose the potatoes. My hope was that there would be enough young potatoes to make it worth while to sacrifice the potato plant as well as a few others in the garden. If the decision was yes, I would run for a bucket and we would dig, clean and pick up new potatoes until there was enough for a meal. My mouth would already be watering just thinking about what would be in store for us at supper that night.

While the delicious taste of my mother's new potatoes certainly justified my excitement, I understand now that part of my excitement was from reaping the rewards of the hard work I had put into growing the potatoes. I knew the potatoes didn't just appear in our garden. It began several months earlier when my father prepared the soil for planting and plowed a furrow for us to plant the potato seedlings. I had helped prepare the seedlings by cutting potatoes into sections, making sure there was at least one eye on each section to send out roots to grow. I had helped plant the seedlings, covering them one by one with a hoe. I had used the same hoe to hoe weeds from the rows so the potato plants could use all the available nutrients and moisture to grow. I had gone up and down each row with a coffee can picking potato bugs off the leaves and throwing them into a can of poisonous gasoline so they wouldn't destroy the plants. It had been hard work and work that I had not particularly enjoyed.

I had made a good deal of sacrifice for those potatoes and that made the reward much sweeter.

At the time I don't believe I realized the significance of the experience. I simply understood if you wanted something you had to work hard and wait for it. A simple concept really, yet one that many adults today still don't grasp. I guess we all have a little bit of the urge to get something without working for it, some of us more than others. I believe it must be innate or the gambling casinos wouldn't be as popular as they are today. However, it's a dangerous attitude to have. The prisons are full of people who wanted to get something without working for it. But if you've been raised on a farm you know something for nothing isn't likely to happen. And, in fact, part of the joy of receiving something is having earned it.

It's important to help children visualize their goals and then teach them how to reach them. Children probably aren't going to be as excited about new potatoes now as I was as a small child. It was a different environment, a simpler time period and my expectations were much less than children have today. However, every child has something they enjoy doing or having. Rather than just giving it to them, teach them what they need to do to earn it. It could be as simple as having them complete their homework before they can watch their favorite TV show or as long-term as cleaning their room for six months before they can have a bicycle. To begin with it should be easy enough to guarantee success.

Once their confidence builds their challenges should be increased as well. Continually teach them how to achieve their goals rather than doing it for them. Praise them for the efforts they put into their work. They need to feel good about the work as well as the reward.

When you have taught them how to visualize their desired future and how to make the necessary sacrifices to reach that future you have given them one of the greatest gifts you can give them as a parent.

"They live well below their means." From the book "The Millionaire Next Door" by Thomas J. Stanley, Ph.D. and William D. Danko, Ph.D.

"How will we survive the hail storm?" My farm experience.

3. SAVE FOR THE FUTURE

The spring of 1963 provided ideal growing conditions for our wheat crop and it looked to be one of the best we had ever had. The wheat was thick and the heads were plump with grain. All we needed were several days of good weather and a record crop would be in the bins ready for sale. After surviving nine months of various hardships the wheat was ready to pay us back for our hard work and investment.

My father and I had just begun the harvest and one truck load was ready for storing when a dark cloud bank appeared on the northwest horizon. It looked like rain so we headed for the shed with the truck to protect the harvested wheat from the moisture. We made it safely but in a short time the rain came. Then small chunks of hail began to fall. Then large chunks of hail began crashing down until the roar on the metal roof of the shed was deafening. The ground became white from the downpour of hail. Within a few minutes it was very obvious that the wheat crop was being destroyed. The wheat plants were being knocked flat to the ground and the wheat heads were being shattered, throwing the grain onto the ground never to be recovered. It was one of those emotional moments that I can still remember vividly. Wheat was our primary source of income and it was now quite clear that there would be little or no income from the wheat crop this year.

I can still remember how amazed I was that my father wasn't more upset. I didn't expect to realize any direct financial benefit from the harvest for myself, but I was still very upset by the loss. I knew my parents needed the money because we were living a relatively modest life style. I knew we had invested a great deal of time and money in the wheat crop and it would never be returned. What I didn't know was that my parents were prepared for just such a disaster. They weren't rich by any means but they had saved enough to survive this disaster.

I know there are many jokes about farmers being conservative and I chuckle about some of them myself. But I think anyone who has spent ten minutes in the shed watching a hail storm destroy a year's income would understand why farmers have to be conservative. I've read that the Mennonite farmers from Russia who first brought winter wheat to Kansas in the 1800's each brought one bag of wheat. Rather than plant it all the first year they only planted 1/3 of the bag in case disaster struck and ruined the crop. Conservative? Yes. Smart? Yes. Saving for the future? Yes.

We survived the hail storm and the loss of our wheat crop. I didn't notice a change in our life style, but then there was never any extravagant spending even in the good years. So a bad year wasn't much different. We prepared the soil for next year's crop and were fortunate to have some good crops in future years. But the lesson I learned served me well in the years to come. Save for the future.

I was to discover later that saving for the future was not just for disasters but for opportunities as well. The savings my wife and I accumulated during the first ten years of our marriage gave me the opportunity to start my own business at age 30. This lead to the financial security we enjoy today.

As I became a member of the city dwellers I was amazed at how little some saved for the future. What seemed natural to me seemed very unnatural to them. One of the first accounts I worked on in the advertising agency where I was employed was a company that rented televisions and stereos to people who wouldn't save enough money to buy one. Some said they were too poor to buy but the fact was if they had only saved their rental payments for a few months they could have bought a TV or stereo. Instead, they were paying for the equipment many times over the actual cost by renting. Saving for the future wasn't a way of thinking they had ever learned and they were destined to always be poor.

Some might say saving money is fine and good, but it takes all the fun out of life. I don't agree. There are plenty of things in life to enjoy, to be passionate about, without spending all of your savings. Look for them, they're all around you. Trying to find happiness by spending too much money is dangerous. You'll likely end up with no money and no happiness.

While saving for the future was a concept easily understood by farm children I think it takes additional effort for city parents to teach the concept to their children. First, of course, parents need to actually be saving for the future themselves. It doesn't do much good to tell children what to do if you aren't doing it yourself. Let them know about your own savings plans, why you are saving, what you are saving for, how you are saving and the ultimate reward for saving. Open a savings account for them at the bank and help them keep records of their savings as they grow.

Help them use their savings wisely. When our own children would see a toy in a TV commercial and announced they wanted to use their savings to buy it, I would say O.K. I would then suggest to them to wait three days and if they still wanted it after that amount of time I would take them to the store to buy it. That satisfied them and, of course, after three days they had usually forgotten about the toy and moved on to other interests. If after three days they still wanted to spend their money I would take them to the store to purchase it because if children think their savings can never be spent they will lose interest in it.

As I recall, my wife used the same technique on me when I fell in love with a boat at the boat show. A few years later we bought the same boat used for substantially less. We all need a little help once in a while.

"Genius is eternal patience." Michelangelo

"Jean finally comes through." My farm experience.

4. IT TAKES THREE YEARS TO GROW A GLASS OF MILK

Our farm was also a dairy farm which meant milking cows every morning and every night. Talk about a commitment. Cows don't stop giving milk on weekends so it becomes a seven day a week job. This fact was one of the reasons I was motivated to get through college. I wanted to graduate and find a job that would allow me weekends off. The idea of having two free days a week seemed like a dream life to me. And avoiding the responsibility to milk the cows every day at 6 A.M. and 5 P.M. would be a life of leisure.

One of the joys of the dairy farm for me as a young child, however, was the birth of calves. They were cute when they were babies and it was fun to watch them grow and develop. We took the calves from their mothers soon after they were born so the mother's milk could be sold to the dairy and a portion saved to feed the calves. As soon as I was big enough to carry a bucket of milk (around 4 or 5 I would guess) my job was to feed the calves morning and night. I gave them all names and watched them grow throughout the year. The males were eventually sold to feeders and the females from the good producing mothers were kept to replenish the dairy herd.

When I was 11 years old it was decided that I should take one of the calves as my own and watch over her development as a 4-H project. 4-H is an organization to instruct young people in useful skills, community service, and personal development.

I named my new calf Jean. She was the daughter of Belle, one of our better producers so there was potential for her to be a good producer. Belle was also a little stubborn and her daughter unfortunately inherited some of those characteristics. I spent many hours trying to teach Jean to be lead by a halter so I could show her at the 4-H fairs. She just didn't feel a need to follow where I was leading. Eventually, my perseverance, patience and determination won out and she agreed to walk along with me most of the time.

After about a year it was time to show her at the 4-H fair competition. Unfortunately, the day before the fair she somehow found a door to the feed bin open and stuffed herself with feed. So much in fact that she became dangerously bloated with her stomach sticking out noticeably. I took her to the fair anyway as the veterinary said it would be safe. I had spent a year getting her ready and didn't want to miss out on the final event. Needless to say she didn't show very well and the judges gave her a white ribbon. I, on the other hand, received a blue ribbon for showmanship. I'm sure the judges must have felt sorry for me for having such a bloated cow and wanted to reward me for my perseverance, determination and patience.

It took another two years before Jean became a mother herself and I might add a very good milk producer. While I had nothing to do with her milk producing prowess I always felt good to know that she was doing so well. It had taken three years before she had produced an ounce of income to the family. It was a lesson in patience I had learned first hand. This was natural and it seemed natural to me. It took time, patience, and care before Jean could begin to pay us back. She was a long-term investment that helped me understand the importance and nature of long-term thinking.

When I see city children today drinking milk I know they have no concept of the time that has been required to grow that glass of milk. All they know is that it comes out of the carton. Perhaps something as simple as a glass of milk is a good place to begin teaching children the concept of long-term thinking. Help them understand that good things take nurturing and time to grow. Help them begin to understand that all good things in life don't just instantly appear. They usually take time, work and patience.

It's difficult, I think, to teach children patience in our modern day city environment. Our lives move so fast now and many things do provide instant gratification. It's easy to fall into the trap of giving our children the things they ask for instantly, thinking that it's a way of showing our love for them. Eventually, though, we must show them some tough love. We must teach them to earn their rewards through work, perseverance, patience, and thinking. If we don't, they'll have difficulty adjusting to the realities of life as they grow older.

Patience, I believe, is a combination of trust, faith and a positive attitude. It can be taught to children through experiences that reward them for their ability to wait for the final reward. It can be as simple as telling a child to sit down and wait for something and you will bring it to them when you have finished your project rather than dropping everything and running to their demands immediately.

Always keep your promises to children. If you think you may not be able to keep it don't make it. It's better to disappoint them in the beginning than to break a promise later. Patience and trust can be broken by a parent who doesn't follow through with a promise made to a child.

Patience will also not be learned by the child who

gets immediate results by throwing a tantrum.   I
know it can be tough not to give in, but if you do it
will only happen more frequently.

"Take care of the goose who lays the golden eggs."
Aesop fable

"You've got to save the terraces to save the soil."
My farm experience.

5. TERRACES

There were many lessons to learn when you were old enough to drive a tractor. Old enough meant tall enough to reach the clutch of the tractor with your outstretched foot. In my case I was around 9 years old. This may sound rather young, but it was fairly normal in the 50's. Young boys were expected to pitch in and help in the fields as soon as possible. Amazingly enough, most of us were eager to do so. I can remember pestering my parents with the question of when I could drive the tractor. Eventually I would get all the tractor driving I wanted, in fact much more than I wanted.

I don't have a clear recollection of my first tractor driving lesson. I'm sure it must have been once around the farm yard and then directly to the field. I do have, however, ingrained into my psyche the instruction "Don't drive over the middle of the terraces!" The thought of doing it today still seems like a sin of unrepairable damage. If I was told once I was told a 100 times that the terraces were built to save the soil from erosion and if I pulled a farm implement over the terraces it would eventually destroy them. These terraces took on the importance of monuments to me. I took great efforts to be sure I didn't knock down any part of the top of the terraces. And if by chance I did accidentally impart some damage to a terrace I felt like I had hurt something very important to our farm. If I had thought there was a terrace God I would have been asking for forgiveness daily.

While the terraces were important they were also difficult to farm. Because the terraces couldn't be crossed it meant that the area between terraces had to be farmed as an individual field. A normal square field became numerous small fields that each had to be worked independently. This added considerable time and effort to completing the job. Even my father would curse the terraces and the inefficiency they caused. But none of us violated their stately position.

The terraces represented a way of thinking, long-term thinking, that was a way of life on the farm. We knew we could farm the land easier without terraces for a few years, but eventually the soil would erode and the land would be damaged. Terraces were expensive to build, but long-term they were necessary. I didn't like the terraces. I didn't like the extra time and work they required. I did, however, respect the terraces and knew they were necessary. At 9 years old I was receiving one of my first and major lessons in long-term thinking.

After graduation from high school I faced the decision of what to do with my life. Some of my friends applied for high paying jobs (at least by my standards) at an area manufacturer and got hired. They started driving new cars and I must admit it looked pretty tempting. But something kept telling me I needed to invest my time and money in an education. I chose to go to college and that lead to the security and independence I enjoy today. There were times in college when I wondered if I had made the right decision. I believe, however, my farm background was telling me I needed to get an education, (build some terraces), for the long-term benefit it would bring to my life. Unlike the character in the Aesop fable who killed the goose to get all the golden eggs at once I was learning to take care of the goose and it would continue to give me golden eggs.

Our own children didn't have the benefit of a terraced field to protect, but they did have a grandfather who knew how to teach them the "Golden Egg" concept. When they were very young my wife's father gave them each a small stock holding in an electric utility that paid quarterly dividends. Each quarter they would receive a dividend check. The checks were for small amounts, but to a 6 year old ten dollars is a large sum of money. It was an ideal way for them to learn through experience that if you take care of the Goose it will continue to give you Golden Eggs. I think it was an excellent teaching method and you can be assured my grandchildren will be receiving quarterly dividend checks.

When children see you taking care of your "Terraces" whether it be your career, education, job, home, business or investments they will begin to understand the concept and benefits of long-term thinking.

"Organize and Execute Around Priorities." From the book "The Seven Habits of Highly Effective People" by Stephen R. Covey

"Get the job done the best and fastest way possible." My farm experience.

6. BECOMING AN EFFICIENCY EXPERT

Of the thousands of hours I worked on the farm I was never once paid by the hour. At the time I felt like slave labor, but I believe it taught me to look at the value of work in a different way than people who have only worked by the hour. I strove to become an efficiency expert on every project I was given. The reward was to get it done as quickly as possible and to do it correctly so I didn't have to do it again. Jobs done incorrectly had a way of showing up again in your life because you lived in and around your work every day.

If I was painting a barn wall I would calculate the best place to start so it would require the least amount of time moving the ladder. If I was working a field I would determine the best method to work it so I would spend the least amount of time possible making unnecessary turns. If I was stacking hay I would determine where each bale should go so it would require the least amount of effort to complete the stack. If I was gathering eggs I would determine the most efficient route to take so I didn't back track any of my steps. I was an efficiency expert by the time I was 12 years old as were most farm children faced with the task of getting a job done. If you want to know the most efficient way to get a project done in your business, ask one of your employees who was raised on a farm. Given some time to study it I would guess they will give you a good answer.

I remember my first job after college required doing a detail project that others had been spending a great deal of time completing. I became quite an annoyance when I kept asking my trainer why were we doing it this way and wouldn't it be better to do it another way. I was told to just do it the way it had been done, so I did until I was on my own. Then I started looking at ways to do it faster just as I had figured out the best route to gather eggs. Efficiency was so ingrained in me that I just had to look for a better way. I did and fortunately my boss took notice. In a few years I was in a management position, still looking for more efficient ways to do things.

Glen Taylor, Chairman and Chief Executive Officer of the Taylor Corporation, related in Forbes Magazine how his farm background helped him make it in the business world.

"Three days after getting out of high school I

walked into Carlson Wedding Services and applied for a job. I thought it was a dress shop, but actually it was a printing place.

I worked on a little press because nobody else wanted to do it. I looked at the press and, probably due to my farm background, decided we could work it a lot faster if we made jigs. So after two weeks on that machine Mr. Carlson noticed that I was printing twice as fast as anybody had ever done in the history of that business.

Then the stock boy wanted to go on vacation for two weeks. I'd never heard of going on vacation for two weeks. I did his job while he was gone and realized how messed up and illogical the inventory was. So I relayed the shelves and straightened out procedures.

When I graduated in 1962 Mr. Carlson asked me to stay on with him. I got a deal with him to buy a minority interest, and then in 1975 I completely bought him out."

I was very pleased when my own city raised son expressed an interest in mowing lawns for money. I had made an effort to pay him by the project rather than by the hour to mow our own lawn. I wanted him to have the experience of working to get the job done rather than thinking about simply being paid by the hour. He and two other boys started a lawn mowing service that summer and made a good deal of money. Of course he wore out my lawn mower in the process but I figured it was one of the best investments I could make in his education.

After I started my own business I added a staff member who was raised in the city and whose first job after college was with a large bureaucratic company. This individual was very hard working and many times took work home. He had elaborate systems set up to do his work and was very proud of his methods. The problem was that the results were very slow in coming. The fact is he had just come from an environment where he had to worry more about looking good in the process than simply getting the job done as efficiently as possible. He had not had the opportunity to learn the benefits of efficient working methods.

As my business grew I always tried to tell my employees that I didn't care how they got the job done, as long as it was done correctly and fast. Obviously there are some limitations to this concept but my observation was that the good employees were much happier when they could do the project in their own way and therefore got it done faster and better.

Certainly it doesn't require being raised on a farm to be efficiency minded. The farm environment does however make it easy to give children projects to do on their own. Look for projects you can give your children to do and then let them figure out the best way to do them. You should give them some guidance, but the best learning will take place when you leave out a few gaps for them to figure out themselves. In addition, they will enjoy the work a great deal more if they have the freedom to be innovative in the way they do it and their self confidence and self esteem will grow. If they are rewarded by the project they will soon look for better, more efficient ways to complete it. It's your job to enforce quality standards to your child's eagerness for efficiency. Efficiency is good but so is quality work. They must learn to do both.

More businesses are recognizing the benefits of efficiency. Employees are being asked for and rewarded for ideas on how the company can be run more efficiently. Unnecessary steps are being removed from procedures because someone is finally asking if this step is really necessary. Computers are opening all kinds of doors to new, efficient procedures. Efficiencies are resulting in profits never seen before in our industries. Even non-profit organizations are discovering the need for efficiencies. It's a wonderful trend that will eventually help everyone.

I believe children who have learned the benefits of efficiency will make more career advancements, help more people, and have more time for family, friends, and community.

"Keep your conscious mind busy with the expectation of the best, and your subconscious will faithfully reproduce your habitual thinking." Dr. Joseph Murphy, D.R.S., Ph.D., D.D., L.L.D. "The Power Of Your Subconscious Mind"

"When you have so much 'alone time' to think, you might as well think the best." My farm experience.

7. TIME TO DREAM

Farming can be a lonely occupation. In fact as a teenager the isolation of farming was the determining factor in my decision to leave the farm. It was not uncommon to spend 10 hours a day on a tractor alone with no one to speak to all day except your immediate family at breakfast, lunch and supper. That gives you a lot of time to your own thoughts. While driving a tractor took some attention it certainly didn't take up the majority of your brain power.

Obviously you become somewhat of a thinker when you spend this much time alone. I would think about my friends, how things worked, how people were different, why people do the things they do, how plants grew, how long it was going to take to finish the field, what I would be doing the next day, week, year, 10 years, 20 years, etc. I would dream about how wonderful it would be to be free to do whatever I wanted to do because in reality I had very little freedom. I found that thinking positive thoughts made the alone time more enjoyable. I had a great deal of time to dream.

I remember watching the airplanes fly over our farm while I was working in the field. We were located on the take off and landing path for the Wichita airport 50 miles north. I would dream that someday I would be in one of those planes far away from the dirt, noise and boredom of working in the field. I had forgotten about that dream until one day 20 years later I was flying on a business trip from Wichita to Dallas and looked out the window at a tractor slowly making its way around a field near my parent's farm. It suddenly occurred to me, here I was just as I had dreamed 20 years ago as a child, high above the ground looking down at someone else working in the field. That dream and so many more dreams I had as a child have come true for me. I've read that thoughts and dreams planted in your subconscious mind have a way of coming to reality and I believe it. You just need to have some time to think and think positively.

I believe it's important for children, and adults, to have time to think and dream. Our fast paced city society leaves little time for either. Some people are turning to meditation, yoga or other relaxation response exercises to give their minds a chance to escape the stresses of everyday life. Unfortunately others turn to alcohol abuse or drugs to escape. Personally, I think they would be better off spending a day working on a farm project alone. The time alone to reflect, be close to nature, and gain the sense of accomplishing something worthwhile would do wonders for most people.

I think it's important for children to be involved in group activities. But I also think they need some alone time to just think and dream. It's more difficult to do in the city because there are so many distractions. My wife recognized this with our children and encouraged them to have some "alone time" away from friends. We also found that reading to the children in bed before they went to sleep was a good time to prepare them for some alone time. They say the best time to plant thoughts in the subconscious is just before sleep. We would read to them from the children's theme encyclopedia of their choice, children's books or make up stories with happy endings. When we would finally leave their bedrooms you could see in their eyes that their imaginations had been stimulated and I'm sure dreams were finding a path to their subconscious.

"Those whose hope is strong see and cherish all signs of new life and are ready every moment to help the birth of that which is ready to be born."
Erich Fromm

"Rejoice in growth for it is life itself." My own thoughts.

8. GROWING PLANTS

As a child I enjoyed riding with my father in the pickup as he inspected the various fields where crops were planted. He would check the plants for insect infestation, probe the soil for moisture content and in general just look at the plants growth progress. As I grew older I would find myself walking to the fields and checking the plants on my own. No one asked me to do this. I found enjoyment in watching the development of the plants week by week.

I believe humans have an innate desire to watch and help things grow. This is an innate desire that I'm sure helped the human race survive over the thousands of years of difficult living conditions. This is a positive human characteristic that has lead to many of the good things we now experience. It's a characteristic that farm children are exposed to by living day to day in a farming environment.

Those of us who were raised in winter wheat growing regions of the country witnessed the growth of one of the hardiest plants in existence. Around the first part of October the fields were prepared for the planting. One last pass over the soil with a farm implement was made to remove any weeds still growing and loosen the soil to receive the seeds. The seeds were then planted in the ground and the waiting process began. Within a few days the seedlings would start to sprout and break their way through the surface of the earth. Brown fields started turning green and each day saw more and more green stems finding their way to the surface. Weather permitting, I would walk or ride my bicycle along the fields on my way to school, a one room school a little over a mile from my home. On the way I would stop to inspect the progress of the plants. It was a joy to watch the greening of the fields. Just as these plants were beginning to get established winter would arrive. Trees and plants all turned brown yet the hardy wheat plants maintained their green color and settled in for the long winter ahead of them. Logic would tell you that they didn't have a chance to survive the bitter cold days ahead of them yet they did.

There wasn't much going on with the wheat during the winter months. It lay dormant, waiting for warm weather and moisture to bring it back to life. By March and April growth would return. It was my favorite time of the year because the wheat was growing rapidly, turning lush and green almost before your eyes. Soon it would be above your ankles, high enough to hide a rabbit. Then the head would begin forming inside the stem and by opening the stem you could see the head in its embryonic state. It was like a miracle to watch these tiny heads form, knowing that in a few more weeks they would shoot out of the stem and eventually ripen into mature wheat. Of course there was no guarantee that weather and insects would let this happen successfully. Green bugs, aphids, army worms, leaf rust, dry conditions, hail, a late freeze were just some of the many things that could harm or destroy the wheat crop. Some of them we could control and some of them we could not. The ones that could be controlled were and the ones that couldn't were simply accepted.

During June, approximately 9 months and a harsh winter after planting, the wheat would be harvested. Even though the plants I had been watching were now dead, it was an exciting time because they were producing seeds that could be sold to support our family and seeds to grow new plants next year. They were not really dying. They were part of an ongoing cycle of wheat. From one seed a plant had grown through harsh conditions to produce many seeds to help others.

Obviously, I didn't think this deeply about

wheat plants as a child. I do, however, believe experiencing the growth of wheat taught me a way of looking at the world that was beyond myself. I witnessed the cycles of life. The birth, growth, development and eventual multiplication of one seed into many seeds. I observed that it takes time and perseverance to grow.

After I left the farm, moved to the city, married and started living in apartments I began to miss being around growing plants. I didn't miss hoeing weeds much but I did miss watching plants grow. One of the first gifts I gave to my wife after we moved into our first apartment was a plant. That was over 30 years ago and we still have the plant to this day, plus several more including off spring of another plant given to us over 30 years ago.

I believe it's important for city children to be exposed to growing plants. In an era when they are primarily exposed to electronic flashes from television, electronic games and CDs it serves as a balance to watch the steady growth and progression of a plant's life. I was pleasantly surprised to hear our 24 year old daughter reminiscing during a recent visit home for Christmas about starting new plants from the stems of our existing house plants when she was a child. She remembered putting the stems in glasses of water, lining them up by the window and waiting for them to shoot out roots. I could tell it had made an impression on her by the vivid description she gave to the moment. Now that she is married and starting a home of her own I believe she is missing watching plants grow too. I would say there's a pretty good chance she'll soon have plants growing in her new home.

"Indeed, keeping our distressing emotions in check is the key to emotional well-being." Daniel Goleman, "Emotional Intelligence".

"Losing control of your emotions can seriously hurt those around you." My farm experience.

9. THE ACCIDENT

Farming is a very dangerous occupation. Working around heavy equipment, powerful tools, large animals and the normal dangers of outdoor labor have taken the lives of many farmers and left others with fingers, arms and legs gone. As young children we were all warned about these dangers but the responsibility of taking care of ourselves was ultimately our own. During the summer of my 14th year I was to learn that taking care of myself and others also meant taking care of my emotions.

The lesson came while my father and I were picking up hay bales from the field. The operation involved attaching a chain driven elevator to the side of the truck. It was slanted at a 45 degree angle so when the truck was driven near a bale it would slide onto the elevator and move its way up to the back of the truck while the truck continued to move forward. The person on the back of the truck would remove the bales from the elevator and stack the bales on the truck. Up to 100 bales could be loaded on a single truck this way by stacking the bales up to 15 feet high. Needless to say this required hard work and good balance on the part of the person stacking the hay while the truck was moving. The truck driver got to avoid the heavy lifting but did have to maneuver the truck carefully to properly feed the bales onto the elevator.

I was 14 years old and still a little unskilled at controlling my temper. I never threw a temper tantrum at my parents (heaven forbid) or other people. However, I could get quite angry at things or objects that didn't do as I wanted. Because there were so many things that could go wrong while working on the farm I had learned how to go from zero to angry in just a few seconds. This, I was to learn, was not a good trait.

The bales we were hauling this particular day were quite large and ragged. This meant many of the bales would hang up on the entrance of the feeding shoot and not slide up the ramp. When this happened I had to stop the truck, put on the emergency brake, get out of the truck, go the the front of the elevator, position the bale correctly, get back in the truck, disengage the emergency bake and move the truck forward again. Doing this once or twice doesn't sound like a big job, but on this particular day I had already done it numerous times when I finally snapped. When one of the bales again refused to go up the ramp I lost my temper and slammed on the clutch and the brake and began to jump out of the truck. At that moment I heard a loud crashing sound on top of the truck cab and then saw my father flying over the hood of the truck and onto the ground. The truck was nearly full and my father had been placing a bale high on the front of the load. When I slammed hard on the brakes the truck stopped but he had no time to balance himself so he fell head first from the top of the fifteen foot high hay stack.

At first he didn't move and I was scared to death I had seriously hurt him or even worse. When I got to him he began to move some and I was glad to know he was alive. I then expected to receive a strong verbal lashing which I knew first hand he was capable of delivering. But he said nothing. That's when I knew it was serious.

He laid there for some time while my mind was racing. What had I done? Had my temper seriously injured my father? Why had I gotten so angry? It seemed like an eternity before he finally spoke. He asked me to help him up and we moved to the truck. He sat there for some time, dazed I'm sure by what had so suddenly happened and probably trying to decide what to say to me. I don't remember to this day what he said. I do know that he didn't yell at me as I expected. I imagine the look on my face told him that I had learned my lesson and additional scolding was really not necessary.

We discovered his shoulder was injured and he couldn't raise his arm above the waist without pain. His head, neck and back seemed to be O.K. so it looked like he had escaped injury to those vital areas.

We made our way to the house, again without much being said. When we entered the house my mother asked what had happen. I told her how I had slammed on the brakes and dad had been thrown off the front of the truck. She looked at me with her piercing eyes and I knew she was both angry and disappointed in me. She did have a few words for me and they weren't pleasant.

My guilt was to last for some time. As most farmers did in those days, he didn't go to the doctor for treatment. He kept his arm close to his side and waited for it to heal. Wheat harvest was only a few weeks away and there was serious concern whether dad would be able to do the work necessary to complete the harvest. My mother was the one who seemed to be the most angry with me and that made my guilt even worse.

Weeks went by and gradually my father's shoulder began to heal. When harvest finally arrived he was still in pain but was able to do the work necessary. He eventually healed with no long term problems, at least none that he mentioned.

I, however, was not the same person I was before the accident. I knew I had let my anger control my judgment. I had lost my temper for an instant and my father had paid the price. I vowed I would not let it happen again.

Learning to control anger is one of the most important skills a child should learn. The prisons are full of people who lost control of their anger and harmed others with their actions. I know how easy it is to lose control and harm someone. I did it.

The farm environment was not a good place to learn anger control for me. I observed my father becoming angry at the many circumstances that went wrong in farm work. Things broke. Things didn't fit right. Animals didn't cooperate. Equipment malfunctioned. Knuckles were scraped. The list goes on and on. I eventually learned my lesson, but it was a dangerous way to learn.

Ultimately I believe children learn much of their emotional characteristics by observing their parents. You can tell them not to loose control of their temper but if they observe you doing it they will adopt the same behavior. Show them you can control your anger and there's a much better chance they will control their anger.

The following excerpt from the book "Emotional Intelligence" by Daniel Goleman, provides some guidance on learning to control anger.

"But timely help can change these attitudes and stop a child's trajectory toward delinquency; several experimental programs have had some success in helping such aggressive kids learn to control their antisocial bent before it leads to more serious trouble. One, at Duke University, worked with anger-ridden grade-school troublemakers in training sessions for forty minutes twice a week for six to twelve weeks. The boys were taught, for example, to see how some of the social cues they interpreted as hostile were in fact neutral or friendly. They learned to take the perspective view of other children, to get a sense of how they were being seen and of what other children might be thinking and feeling in the encounters that had gotten them so angry. They also got direct training in anger control through enacting scenes, such as being teased, that might lead them to lose their temper. One of the key skills for anger control was monitoring their feelings, becoming aware of their body's sensations, such as flushing or muscle tensing, as they were getting angry, and to take those feelings as a cue to stop and consider what to do next rather than strike out impulsively."

This appears to be scientific proof of the old adage of "count to ten" before you react. I took this concept a little further in my business career. When angered by a client or supplier I would write my thoughts in a letter to them and then hold it for a day before sending it. After 24 hours I would usually find the letter to be inappropriate and not send it or make drastic changes before mailing. This technique saved me from making some terrible mistakes.

Certainly holding all anger inside is not good for mental health. The trick is to learn how to vent it in appropriate ways. For children that means explaining and showing them what is acceptable and what is not acceptable. It means teaching them how to resolve conflicts and problems with logic rather than diving in with uncontrolled emotions. Spending some time on this with children when they are young is time well spent. If you don't, you'll be spending a great deal more time helping them deal with problems they create for themselves with uncontrolled anger in later years.

As Aristotle stated in "The Nicomachean Ethics", "Anyone can become angry, that is easy. But to be angry with the right person, to the right degree, at the right time, for the right purpose, and in the right way, that is not easy."

"Begin with the end in mind." Habit # 2 from the Stephen Covey book, "The 7 Habits of Highly Effective People."

"What will they be saying about me?" My rural experience.

10. THE CEMETERY

It was the summer of 1963 and I was a 15 year old boy. By now I was a well experienced farm hand and could tackle just about any job thrown at me. My confidence was high and I knew all the answers. I felt like I had the respect of my grandfather and parents as a hard worker who could be trusted to get the job done right and fast. I felt I was indestructible.

The knock on the door came at 6 A.M. with the message that my grandfather had suffered a heart attack and was in serious condition. He was a giant of a man in my eyes and I just couldn't imagine anything happening to him. My father rushed to the hospital and my mother and I stayed home to take care of the chores, hoping that he would survive the attack. He didn't.

The funeral was a large one for my grandfather had lived in the farm community all of his life. His parents and grandparents had also lived in the community, homesteading there in the late 1800's. The final step of the funeral took us all to the country cemetery where my grandfather was to be buried.

The cemetery was located 10 miles from the nearest town. It was surrounded by trees from a nearby creek and pasture, a setting unique to the treeless plains of south central Kansas. The nearest road of any consequence was 1/2 mile away so there was no traffic noise, no industrial noise, no noise of any kind other than the occasional chirp of a bird and the breeze making its way through the trees. It was definitely a setting for reflecting on my grandfather's life and to many of us, our own lives.

After the ceremony, well wishers came to the family to express their sympathy and convey their admiration for my grandfather. He was held in high regard in the community for his integrity, farming success and willingness to help neighbors in need. By listening to people talking among themselves I could tell their feelings were genuine and not just idle sympathy comments for family members to hear.

Older members of the family then began making the usual pilgrimage made when visiting the family cemetery. First it was to the grave sites of my great grandfathers and grandmothers Harris, Overholt and Kreider who had lived and raised their families only a few miles from the cemetery. Then, on to the gravestones of my great, great grandfathers and grandmothers Osburn and Kreider who had homesteaded and raised their families close to the cemetery. At the time I didn't know much about these families but I did know they were well respected.

I felt a new sense of responsibility that day as I walked among the graves of the three previous generations of my family. It was a feeling that was new to me as a 15 year old boy. It was an awareness that I needed to think beyond what I was going to be doing next Saturday night with my friends. I realized, I think, for the first time that while I was only 15 years old, I too would someday be following the paths of my ancestors. People would be gathering for my funeral someday, reviewing what my life had meant to them. It was the beginning of a way of thinking that would be a positive influence on me the rest of my life. It's a way of thinking identified by Stephen Covey in his book "The 7 Habits of Highly Effective People" as Habit 2 "Begin With The End In Mind." In his best selling book he asks his readers to visualize speakers at their own funeral answering questions such as, "What kind of husband, wife, father, or mother would you like their words to reflect? What kind of son or daughter or cousin? What kind of friend? What kind of working associate? What character would you like them to have seen in you? What contributions, what achievements would you want them to remember? Look carefully at the people around you. What difference would you like to have made in their lives?"

Certainly it's not necessary to be raised on a farm to begin this way of thinking. Many city families have passed this way of thinking on to their children through conscious effort. I do however believe the typical farming community makes this lesson one that is learned through simple osmosis. Most farm communities have a community cemetery where several generations of the family are buried. Families tended to stay in one community so there is a feeling of continuity carried forward to your own life and actions. And the family cemetery makes it quite obvious that you too will be joining the generations ahead of you someday. The obvious concern upon reaching this conclusion is; "What will they be saying about me? Was he a good person? Was he helpful to others? Was he successful at his work?"

How is a city family to help their children learn the concept of beginning with the end in mind without the benefit of the farm/rural culture? I believe it needs to be done through what children see and hear in their daily lives. Sitting them down and giving them one big lecture and then forgetting about it probably won't do much good. Rather, whenever an opportunity presents itself to admire the positive characteristics of someone deceased or living, family or friend, be sure to do it in front of the children. You don't have to tell them you want them to take on the positive characteristics. The fact that you are admiring those characteristics lets them know you consider them to be important.

Our mobile society is making the family cemetery a thing of the past. In many ways, however, I believe a family history photo album can serve as a replacement. It can provide the catalyst to present positive stories about ancestors. Notice I said positive. Most of us have ancestors who weren't perfect all the time. None of us are. Dwelling on their short comings will only be hurtful to you and your children. This is the time to accentuate the positive. These observations will begin to help children realize that people's character does in fact continue to live on after their death through the memories of those who knew them or knew about them. Hopefully, they will then live lives that allow them to feel good about the question; "What will they be saying about me?"

"Treat others as you would like to be treated" The Golden Rule

"Always try to do more for others than they've done for you." My father's advice on helping neighboring farmers.

11. HELPING OTHERS

It was the summer of 1964 and we had just completed plowing the ground from the recently completed harvest. Plowing is probably one of the most boring, dreaded and time consuming jobs a farm child had to accomplish. The plow covered a narrow area of ground so it took weeks of 14 hour days to complete the plowing. Around and around the field you would slowly go seeing only small accomplishments after a day's work. It was usually hot, dirty and the noise from the tractor was deafening. Needless to say when our plowing was done we were all sick of plowing and ready for a break.

We finished the last field in the morning and it was such a relief to come in for lunch knowing the plowing was done. You can imagine how I felt when my dad announced at lunch, "Let's go help George finish plowing." After a few moments of disbelief I thought to myself, "You've got to be kidding. George has never done anything for us.

Why should we go help him?"

George was an old farmer who had lived in the community for years. He was not what you would call a progressive farmer, but he did do a commendable job of farming his two quarters of land with his single small tractor. Even though his farm was 1/2 mile from our home we could easily see his almost torturously slow progression toward completion of his plowing. My parents would watch his progress and comment on how poor old George was never going to get done. Even though I was suffering through the same plowing nightmare I did feel a little sorry for him. But to go help him for no reason at all was not something I would have come up with on my own. But help him we did.

I can still remember the look on his face when we pulled into his field with our tractors and plows. I'm sure it must have looked like an unimaginable dream come true to him. With our tractors and his we finished his plowing that evening and he could go home and rest. He was smiling from ear to ear and was so appreciative of our help. I too was smiling as I drove the tractor home that evening. It was a good feeling to have helped the old man. I didn't expect him to ever pay us back and that was O.K. with me. We had helped him with no strings attached and that made it feel even better. I never enjoyed plowing much but I did enjoy that afternoon helping old George.

Helping your neighbors was and still is part of the basic value system in most farm communities. If someone was sick, injured or there was a death in the family, the neighbors were there to help. As a young boy it seemed to me like my dad was extra eager to help others. I asked him once why we were always going to help someone else. He told me it was important to be sure you had done more for others than they had done for you. I accepted what he said but I was still a little skeptical, that is until the summer harvest of 1980.

I had just started my business and was working day and night to get it off the ground. My wife and I had two young children that took up any spare time I could find. Then I received the call. My mother called to tell me that Dad had suffered a stroke and they were bringing him to the hospital for observations. I called my wife, took care of the absolute necessities in my office and raced to the hospital to meet them. For the first time in my life I saw my father frightened. As he told me later, he wasn't afraid of dying, he was afraid of losing the ability to lead an active life. The doctors began running tests and determined that no long-term serious damage had been done. After several days he was sent home to rest and recuperate.

Within a few days I received another frantic call from my mother telling me that Dad was on the combine heading to the field to harvest wheat. She had pleaded with him to stay in the house and rest but the call for harvest and the typical male stubbornness was more than she could overcome. She pleaded with me to come to the farm and do something. Again I took care of the absolute necessities and headed to the farm. He wasn't about to stop but he did agree to let me run the combine while he rested in the truck. The call came on a Friday, so the approaching weekend allowed me to come to the farm and continue running the combine. I didn't know what I was going to do on Monday. Harvest could last for weeks at this rate and my new business was demanding that I be there to service my clients. I really had no choice. I would work in my office early in the morning and go to the farm in the late morning when the sun had dried the moisture off the wheat so it could be harvested. We would harvest the rest of the day and into the night. Hopefully we would get done in a few weeks, before my dad had over exerted himself and I had lost any clients.

I called the farm late Monday morning to see if the wheat was dry enough to harvest. My mother answered the phone with a sparkle in her voice that I hadn't heard for some time. She said, "You won't believe what has happened. All the neighbors brought their combines over this morning and the elevator agreed to accept the wheat even though it wasn't completely dry and our harvest is done!

There were so many of them they were done in just a few hours!" I couldn't believe what I was hearing. Harvest was a critical time for all the area farmers yet they had taken time away from their own harvest to come help my father and mother. Then my father's words came back to me. " Always try to do more for others than they've done for you." It looked like he was right. Our family had always been one of the first to help others in need and it was apparent they were eager to try to balance the scale.

My father recovered and continued to farm and search out ways to help others until his death 6 years later. Again, the neighbors came to harvest my mother's wheat for her.

I don't know if my father died with his scales balanced toward giving or receiving. I know his intent would have been toward the giving side but it doesn't really matter. The important thing was that he and my mother taught us that it was more important to give than to receive.

I carried this helping attitude into my own business without really realizing where it came from at the time. I always tried to help my clients more than they were expecting. I tried to give them more than they were paying for. I believe that attitude was important to the success I was able to achieve.

I placed a plaque on the wall of my office

reception area that I believe my mom and dad would have appreciated. It states "The rewards go to people who search diligently for ways to help others."

It's difficult to teach children the importance of helping people while living in the city environment. Neighbors come and go before you hardly have a chance to meet them. The sense of community just isn't there when everyone in the neighborhood has different jobs and seldom see each other. The pace of life is much faster and people don't feel they have the time to devote to helping others. Schools are the primary community activity but even they are becoming less community oriented with busing, magnet schools and private schools.

Churches are left as the primary organization left to show children the concept of helping others. I believe church experience is important during a child's formative years. The church usually plays a major role in most rural/farm communities and many of the lessons learned from a farm background can be traced to the teachings of the church.

"Talk to your children while they are eating; what you say will stay even after you are gone." Nez Perce, Native American Proverb.

"Every meal was a family meal." My farm experience.

12. FAMILY MEALS

Much of farm life was unpredictable. If it rained the day's plans were changed. If a piece of equipment broke the plans changed. If an animal became sick the plans changed. However, there was one very predictable event that you could count on, the family meal.

After the cows were milked in the early morning, we all had breakfast together. When noon came we all left the projects we were working on and came to the house for lunch (we called it dinner). After the cows were milked in the evening we all had dinner together (we called it supper). Psychologists today are expounding on the importance of the family having meals together. It's a time for the family to be together, to bond, to share ideas, experiences, and values. It provides an atmosphere that I believe is very important to the development of children. For our family it was a necessary fact of life. We ate every meal together because there was no other choice. I don't believe my parents had read any psychological studies about the importance of family meals. It was just the natural thing to do.

It was at these family meals that I learned about my parents' values. They didn't necessarily direct their conversations to us children. We mostly listened. We learned how they admired a neighbor who helped someone in need. We heard how they admired a particularly hard worker in the neighborhood. We learned how the payments on the farm would be completed in a few years and they would own the farm free and clear, we learned about the lives of our extended family, we heard about the activities our parents were involved with in the community, we answered questions asked about our lives, we asked questions about things we didn't understand, we heard about the plans they were making for the next few days, weeks, months and years. It was the focal point for the passing of information, ideas and values from parents to children. It was a good thing and it happened naturally.

Today it is very difficult for city families to have family meals together. It takes special efforts by the parents to make it happen. I've been blessed to have a wife who understood the importance of the family meal, more so than I did during the time our children were home. It was not easy for her to accomplish the family meal, but she made a concentrated effort to make it happen. My work schedule would sometimes conflict, children's after school events conflicted, invitations from children's friends conflicted, her activities conflicted. It was a constant battle, but she accomplished it as much as possible. The television was turned off. I must confess that I complained a few times about this myself when the meal came in the middle of a show I was watching but in my heart I knew it was the right thing to do. When we only had a chance to have maybe one meal a day together it was important to focus on that time together.

Work at making the meal time a positive experience for everyone. It's not the time to bring up negative subjects or the children will soon dread coming to the meal. It's a time for sharing information, ideas and values. It's a time for listening to what others have to say. It's a time for supporting each other. It's a time for talking about and looking forward to the future.

"More people lose their positions and their big opportunities in life because of the inability to cooperate with others than for all other reasons combined." Napoleon Hill, "Think and Grow Rich"

"When there are only 12 children in your entire school, you better get along with everyone if you want to have any friends." My rural experience.

13. GETTING ALONG WITH OTHERS

You'll find that most people with a farm background are pretty easy to get along with. One of the primary reasons I believe is because we were isolated and had few opportunities to be with other children so when we had a chance to be with them we made the most of it.

The one room grade school I attended usually had approximately 12 students for the year. This covered all 8 grades so there was an average of only 1 or 2 per grade. Consequently, if you wanted to have any friends you had to get along with everyone. It didn't matter if they were boy or girl, older or younger, smarter or slower, richer or poorer. We all got along, played games together, got in trouble together and learned together. We learned how to get along with each other despite our differences.

When I reached high school and discovered there were 30 students in my class, 120 in the total school, I thought I was in heaven. I saw it as an opportunity to make 120 new friends. The other freshmen town boys were in shock when they saw me talking to the senior girls. It was an age barrier they saw as unbreakable. For me it only seemed natural. One of my best female friends in my one room school was three years older than me so I saw no reason why I shouldn't be talking to the senior girls. What the other boys saw as courage beyond imagination was to me only being friendly.

As I entered the work world of advertising and marketing consulting I discovered my background of getting along with all kinds of people was very helpful. On any given day I might be working with creative staffs, warehouse workers, sales people, accountants, marketing managers or the CEO of a large corporation. Sometimes all in the same day. These transitions were easy for me and I believe a good deal of the reason is due to my childhood experience. This ability, I believe, contributed significantly to the success I was able to achieve in the business world.

The environment was different for our own children. There were so many children in the area their own age I seldom saw them playing with children older or younger than themselves. They also had the option to only be friends with children who were very similar to themselves. When there were 300 children in their class they naturally gravitated to the children who were similar.

I believe the only way city parents can counter this tendency is to expose the children to as many sub-groups as possible. Groups such as Boy Scouts, Girl Scouts, athletic teams, Sunday School, and hobby groups provide an opportunity for children to experience different types of people. These groups also teach them how important it is to get along with other people and work together. We kept our children busy in numerous groups outside of school and were there to encourage and support them in these activities. I'm happy to say they both have the ability to "get along" with others.

"Doubly rich is the man still boyish enough to play." Charles R. Wiers

"Let's go to the lake."   My parents

14. TAKE TIME FOR FUN

I know it sounds like being raised on the farm was mostly work and we did do a great deal of work. However, I was also blessed with parents who saw the benefit of having some fun too. They chose boating and water skiing as the family activity we would enjoy. I'm sure they didn't research with a psychologist to determine what would be a good family activity but I don't think they could have selected a better form of family entertainment. It began with a small wooden used boat with a 25hp motor that would barely pull an adult skier up out of the water. Three families went together to buy the boat to see how much the families would enjoy it. Before long it was obvious that boating and skiing was a big success and the other two families bought bigger, new boats. We kept the original wooden boat and upgraded to a little bit bigger motor. Eventually, my father couldn't stand it any longer and bought a bigger, faster fiberglass boat. Of course he bought a used one to save money.

Our boating days were usually reserved for

Sundays. They began with early morning chores, then a trip to church for Mother, my brother and me. Upon returning home Dad would have the boat ready and Mom would hurriedly prepare a picnic lunch. If friends had been invited they would soon arrive and away we would go to the lake. Even though we may have been exhausted from the last 6 days of work we would find new energy at the lake. It was a great escape from the dirt and work of the farm.

I think most kids are amazed when they see their parents having fun and acting like children. Certainly when you work with your parents every day in a work environment seeing them having carefree fun presents them in a new light.

I believe it's important for children to see their parents having fun. If children only see their parents working day after day and finding no real enjoyment in life they will become cynical to the whole process. They may drop out and start looking for forms of pleasure, many times the wrong kind in the wrong places.

It doesn't matter what the activity is but ideally it should be something you can do as a family and everyone enjoys. In our case boating and skiing were ideal. It provided the excitement and daring that appealed to my brother and me. It provided the picnic environment my mother enjoyed. It provided my father with the excitement of water skiing and the opportunity to watch his sons grow and improve. Most importantly it provided an environment where the entire family was brought together in close proximity to enjoy life together. No televisions, phones, work or other distractions to separate us. It was a time for my brother and me to see our parents in a different light. We saw them not as rule makers or bosses from work, we saw them as other human beings having a fun time.

Eventually the same boat would be used to teach our own two children how to water ski. My parents took great joy in watching their grandchildren learn to ski and our children looked forward to the outings with great anticipation. We eventually bought our own boat and carried on the same family tradition with our children. Our children are now grown and gone but I know some of their fondest memories are the times we spent boating together. Maybe I'll have the opportunity to help teach my own grandchildren how to water ski some day. Wouldn't that be grand!

There are many activities families can enjoy together. I think the important point is to find something everyone can enjoy doing. Children need to learn they can have fun with their parents without alcohol, doing drugs, taking dangerous risks or taking part in anti-social activities. It's one of the more enjoyable responsibilities of a parent, teaching your children how to have fun!

"Work is the true elixir of life. The busiest man is the happiest man. Excellence in any art or profession is attained only by hard and persistent work." Sir Theodore Martin

"Work was the focal point of our farm life." My farm experience.

15. WORK ETHIC

It was the summer of my 12th year and it was near the end of the plowing season. I was being entrusted to drive the big tractor with the four bottom plow for the first time. We needed to get the plowing done so it was determined by my dad that I would drive the big tractor during the day and my older brother would run it during the night so we could keep it running constantly to finish the plowing sooner. My dad started me on a 10 acre field after lunch and told me my brother would be back to take over that evening. For some reason he told me I would probably only have the field about half done. I didn't say anything to him but I took it as a challenge to have the field more than half done when they returned.

I spent the entire afternoon doing everything I could to speed up the plowing process. I never stopped once to take a drink of water, choosing instead to drink while the tractor was moving. I drank such little water that the need to stop to relieve myself was not necessary. I cut the corners as sharp as possible rather than taking the necessary time to round them for a smoother finish. When I did round the corners I did it as fast as I could without harming the tractor or myself.

When my father and brother returned to the field I was nearly two thirds done and they were both astonished at what I had accomplished. While my dad noticed the corners were a little rough, he showed far more praise for my accomplishment than for my lack of tidiness. Even my brother was complimentary of the amount of ground I had covered, although the fact that it meant there was less for him to do might have had something to do with his excitement.

I felt like a war hero as my father drove me home from the field that evening. I had been sent out to do battle with time and the ground and I had won!

What would drive a 12 year old to this level of determination about his work? Being a good worker was how I won praise and how I felt good about myself. The folklore about my ancestors was primarily about their work accomplishments and I felt like I was earning my place in the family history.

I can recall as a child hearing the family talk about those who were good workers and those who weren't. I knew that if I wasn't a good worker I wouldn't be looked upon as a good person by my family. In a sense my self-worth and positive identity were directly related to how good a worker I was.

While I was the fifth generation of the family to live in the area since my ancestors homesteaded their farm, the necessity of hard work to survive as a homesteader was still being passed down to my generation. Conditions were harsh for the early homesteaders and they had to work hard just to survive. Their children were taught that hard work was honorable and necessary. They in turn passed the concept down to their children and so it continued to be passed all the way down to me. While many Midwesterners have moved to the city by necessity, a good percentage of them have ancestors who were raised on a farm and taught their children that being a hard worker was a positive trait. Thus the present day Midwestern work ethic is only a few generations away from its farm roots.

I also believe that because farm families live in and around their work everyday, all day, it's hard to ignore a job not done well. If you plant a crooked row, fail to repair a fence correctly, fail to work the ground in a timely manner, your errors are very visible to everyone in your family and to the community. You also learn that if you don't fix a problem right the first time it will come back to haunt you later. It's easy to see how the Midwestern work ethic developed and why it is such a wonderful trait to have in an employee or business relationship.

As I've aged and moved to the city, I find myself questioning the wisdom of devoting too much of your time to work. It was effective on the farm because the family generally worked together, but in the city, work usually takes you away from your family. We've all heard the stories of a man who devoted himself to his business only to find when he reached success that his wife and children were gone because he had ignored them over the years. Obviously, that's not the end result any of us want from our efforts.

My observation of people who work in the city is there can be a big difference between working hard and just working many hours. It's easy to fall into the habit of postponing difficult or unpleasant tasks, telling yourself you will do them in the evening or on the weekend. It's also easy to not work as hard and as efficiently as possible during the day thinking that if I don't get a project done I'll finish it tonight or on the weekend. My advice would be to avoid these habits as best you can and to work focused, efficiently and as hard as possible during the working hours of your day. Tackle those difficult tasks and get them out of the way as soon as possible. When it's time to go home to your family, go home, leave work behind and focus on family and home activities with as much intensity as possible. I know from my own experience this is easier said than done and there will be times when work responsibilities overwhelm you. The important point is to not let it become a habit and way of life. Strive to get back in balance as soon as possible.

Is it possible for city children to learn the good work ethic habits farm children are exposed to every day? Of course it is, but I do think it takes special efforts by the parents because the environment is so much different. As opposed to the farm environment where the parent's work is very visible, many city children really don't know or understand what kind of work their parents do. Work just means they're gone from home.

I think it's important to take your children to your work place and explain to them what you do. Show them the results of your work and explain the importance of your work to the overall success of the business and how it helps other people. Place importance on your work beyond just bringing home a pay check. Children need to feel that work has importance in itself. Present what you do in a positive manner. If you display disgust for your job and the work you do children will believe that work is a bad thing.

Praise your children for working hard on a task. Even if they've made an error or two, place value on the fact they have focused on a project.

I think the ultimate work ethic killer is continually giving people something without them having earned it. Certainly gifts are appropriate and sometimes people need a helping hand to get back on their feet. But continually giving things to people who haven't earned them only destroys their self-image and their work ethic.

I recently saw a sign in a national forest that said "Don't feed the Bears." The reason given was that if people give the bears food they will eventually forget how to forage for their own food and will become a dangerous nuisance in their search for handouts and free food. Apparently we can destroy the work ethic in animals too.

It's usually easier to give someone something than to teach them how to earn it themselves. If you really care about them, you will take the time to teach them how to earn it themselves.

"If two people have the same ability, the one that's the best public speaker will be given the promotion." My business experience

"There's no need to be afraid of speaking at the community meeting. They're all your friends." My farm experience

16. PUBLIC SPEAKING

One of the primary social events in a one room school farm community was the monthly community meeting. It was a wonderful time when people in the community all came together at the school house for an evening of business, refreshments, socializing, and entertainment. I don't remember much about the business part but I do remember the entertainment and refreshments part. Some months the children in the school would prepare a program for the adults. It might involve a theatrical play, music or individual performances. It was such an important part of our community that an abandoned school was moved to our school to be used as a room addition for a stage. As I recall the new addition eventually included indoor restrooms for the first time. Yes, prior to that we had no indoor plumbing.

Individuals from the community also took this opportunity to perform. Those who could play a musical instrument were always popular on the invitation list. Since my mother was a good pianist she was often called upon to help with the entertainment. And occasionally that meant my brother and I were called upon to be part of the performance. I became very accustomed to speaking in front of a group of people through the school performances and my mother's performances. It was an experience that my brother and I were both to learn in later life was a blessing.

My mother also encouraged us to participate in the 4-H Club speech and demonstration competition on a county-wide basis. This was a little more serious because we would be giving a demonstration in front of a group of people who were mostly strangers and would be judged on how well we did. I remember being somewhat more nervous about these presentations. However, the countless hours of practice my mother put me through meant that I was well prepared and did a good job. Her help in writing the speeches and demonstrations was an obvious plus. I don't recall ever receiving any award less than a blue ribbon at these county-wide events. My confidence in speaking to groups was definitely growing.

It goes without saying, my mother was a tremendous influence on my brother and me. She was both creative and disciplined. She taught us communication skills and encouraged us to spread our wings and look beyond the farm. The seeds she planted in us lead to my successful career in the advertising industry and my brother's successful career in radio/television/movies.

Being raised on a farm might not sound like the ideal place to learn to be comfortable with public speaking. In reality it was an ideal place. The opportunities were there through the community meetings and 4-H activities. The audiences at the community meetings were friendly and the performances at the county level provided the ideal opportunity for a more serious experience. Of course high school and college provided the opportunity and learning experience to further develop these skills. However, I believe the performance experiences we had as children provided the most important ingredient, confidence.

My own career and advertising agency business benefited greatly from this background. The turning point in my career came when I was asked by my client to prepare and present a presentation to a large group of independent pharmacists on how they could unite and work together for a better future. The CEO heard my speech and within a few days I was being invited to join the company and head up this project. I rejected this offer because I wanted to be independent, but did suggest I would help them develop the project as an outside contractor. They accepted the offer and that decision made all the difference in the world. It lead to the success of my own advertising agency.

My brother's big career move came as the result of someone hearing him give a speech about the feasibility of establishing a 4th television network. He was offered a job at Paramount Movie Studios and later became president of the television division of Paramount. Eventually, he moved on to become president of Sony Pictures, one of the top positions in Hollywood.

It's easy to see why I believe teaching children to be comfortable speaking and performing in front of groups is important.

Children raised in the city may not have the security of the neighborhood community meeting or 4-H to learn the confidence needed for public speaking, however there are many avenues open to them. As a parent I believe it is important for you to encourage your children to have these experiences.

Our own children began to learn about public speaking because of my own thrifty farm background. It began when a neighbor hired a magician to entertain the children at her child's birthday party. My wife suggested we do the same and I said it was ridiculous to pay a magician

$40.00. So I volunteered to be the magician. I made a trip to the novelty store and found several tricks that I thought I could perform for our five year old daughter and her friends and at a cost of much less than $40.00 I might add. My magic tricks turned out to be a big hit and our three year old son got his first taste of public appearance by being my assistant. It became a birthday tradition and I became known as the "Magic Man" to my children's friends. What fun it was.

After a few more "Magic Man" appearances our daughter and her friends were wanting to put on a show of their own. I was delighted. They prepared a play of their own, complete with costumes created from their play clothes. Our basement, the location where the "Magic Man" usually appeared, was prepared for a theatrical presentation. Parents of all the children were invited one evening and seated in rows of chairs just like the theater. Their performance was magnificent. The applause from the parents brought smiles to their faces and they had begun to gain the confidence that is so important in public presentations.

When our children were old enough to attend school there were plenty of opportunities for them to make public appearances and with some encouragement from my wife, who was more involved in the school activities than me, they both appeared in school plays with major roles.

It has paid off in spades. Our daughter has won numerous awards from her employer in her career as a professional sales representative. Our son's employer has recognized his "natural ability to make presentations" and is moving him toward a management/leadership position. This was no surprise to me. I've seen it happen so many times in my life.

Encourage your children to be involved in activities that require them to be public speakers. It could be Sunday School, Boy Scouts, Girl Scouts, school, sporting events or just family gatherings. If there's a family prayer before meals, let the children give it once in a while. It will build their confidence and help them achieve what they want in life.

"Buy low and sell high." Anonymous

"The 80 acres paid for itself in one year." My farm experience.

17. INVESTMENTS

During the spring of 1960 the wheat crop looked like it was going to be a dismal failure. A poor sprouting in the fall and a harsh winter had left a very thin stand of wheat for spring growth. And then a miracle began to happen. Growing conditions turned ideal and the experiment of using more fertilizer put the plants into a super growth mode. The plants grew additional stalks and the wheat heads filled with an extra row of berries. The final crop on our farm averaged 50 bushels to the acre, far above the average during that time period. The market price for wheat was also above normal so it was a very good year financially.

It was a time of celebration. I had never seen my father so happy and proud of his accomplishment. During one of his moments of exuberance, he announced that the 80 acres of land he and my mother had purchased 8 years earlier would generate enough income from this crop to cover the total purchase price of the land.

While the crop was substantial, the main reason the crop was able to pay for the land was because it was not very desirable land 8 years earlier and they had purchased it at a low price. Through my father's care of the land by terracing, planting clover, spreading manure, and fertilizing, the poor soil was producing amazing results. It became an investment that paid for itself many times over.

While I was only 12 at the time, I was getting my first lesson in investing. The lesson was to buy undervalued properties or companies that have good potential for increased value and income, be patient and the rewards will follow.

It was many years later before my wife and I had any money left over for investing. I was busy with my career and family so I had little time to study investments. It was the early seventies and mutual funds were just beginning to gain attention so I investigated them. They looked like a good way for us to get professional investment help at a relatively low expense. Further investigation revealed two types of funds that caught my attention. One group was called "go-go" funds and they focused on a high risk-high reward style. A second group, called value funds, focused on undervalued stocks that appeared to have long-term growth potential. My instinct told me to put it all in a well managed value fund, but being young I still had the urge to get rich quick with a "go-go" fund. I chose to divide the money with one half going to the best value fund and one half going to the best "go-go" fund.

The seventies were a terrible time to be in the stock market and I soon lost interest. Eventually I did start paying attention again and noticed the value fund had continued to steadily grow while the "go-go" fund was actually worth less than I paid for it. So I began putting more and more money in the value fund. Even during bad market times the value fund soon regained any losses, giving me the confidence to continue to invest. It's amazing how an investment can grow with the combination of steady investing and time. I'm surprised more people haven't discovered how simple this really is. Yes, there are some risks involved but my experience is the risks are minimal when you invest in a well managed value fund. The benefit is that the low volatility of the value funds encourage you to continue to invest on a regular basis. And regular, continuous investing is the key to success.

Even though I received a good lesson in investing when I was 12, I must admit I have made my share of horrible mistakes. Most were based on the concept I was going to make a good deal of money in a short period of time. I should have known better. I do now. The fact is few people are fortunate to find a get-rich quick investment that works. Far more lose part or all of their investment.

When you explain to your children that an investment making 12% a year will double in only 6 years they'll see why time is the critical ingredient. A $10,000.00 investment in a tax deferred account earning 12% a year will grow to $320,000.00 in 30 years. They may not be getting rich quick, but they will be getting rich.

As my father-in-law likes to quote to his grandchildren, the secret is to invest and "make money while you sleep." I believe that concept is a good one for everyone to learn.

"A little competition is a good thing and severe competition is a blessing." Jacob Kindleberger

"It was important to practice and do the very best you could do." My farm experience.

18. COMPETITION

It was the summer of my twelfth year and it was suggested I should enter the tractor driving contest held by our county 4-H clubs. I don't remember who had the idea I should compete, but I do remember my parents wanted me to practice if I entered the contest. Thank goodness they did or it would have been a disaster.

I had never been to the event and had no idea of what to expect, but my parents thought it was a good idea so I decided to do it.

I was told the contest consisted of two parts. The first part was to drive a tractor pulling a harrow through a narrow lane of markers with circles at both ends of the lane. The second part was to back a tractor and two wheel trailer through a series of barrels and into a mock shed. It was determined I didn't need to practice the harrow pulling part of the contest since I already had plenty in experience of working with that type of farm implement. The trailer backing was another matter. I had no experience in this area and needed help in a big way.

Practicing entailed going to my uncle's farm because we didn't own a two wheel trailer. Ours was a four wheel model. Once there I was given a wide open area to practice and I needed all the space I could get. Backing was an experience I had never had before and my initial response was to over steer to correct any errors I made. The result was a series of sharp turns that left me far from my intended course. It was determined by those watching that I needed some guidance. My dad took over the coaching job.

He told me the secret to backing was to look into the distance where you wanted to go and then make only slight adjustments in steering to reach the goal. He told me that looking only at the trailer would cause me to loose sight of the direction I wanted to go and cause me to make a series of short jerky moves that would get me way off track. (Very similar to the advice I had received in planting straight rows. Focus on where you want to go and make adjustments until you get there. It's good advice for directing your life as well). I took his advice and in a short period of time was backing the trailer very well. I was amazed at how easy it was when I did it the correct way. After more practice it was determined by my father, uncle and grandfather I was ready for the contest.

When the day of the contest arrived I was eager

to participate. I guess I should have been nervous, but I saw it as a chance to show others what I had learned. When we arrived at the event and I saw the obstacle courses I did begin to get nervous. They were much harder than I had expected. The harrow pulling segment involved pulling a harrow through a row of obstacles (bricks) with only a few inches of clearance on each side. The most difficult part was you then had to circle around and come back into the row without hitting a brick during the circling process. It was much harder than I had expected.

When my turn arrived my dad gave me one last word of instruction. He told me not to look at the bricks, instead, keep my eyes on the center of the row. He told me to look and drive toward the center of the row because if I took my eyes off it and looked at the obstacles I would get off track and start hitting them. (It's good advice for living your life too. Focus on where you want to go, not on the obstacles.) I took his advice and kept a steady eye and hand toward the center of the lane. When I completed the course I wasn't sure how I had done because I had purposely not looked back to see if I had hit any bricks. My dad was smiling from ear to ear when I got off the tractor and informed me I had not hit a single brick. His advice had worked well for me.

Points were deducted for each brick hit on the

course so I was sitting with a perfect score going into the backing contest. A few others had managed to get through with a perfect score so it looked like the backing contest would be the deciding factor.

The backing course was also much more difficult than I had expected. It consisted of backing a trailer back and forth through a line of four barrels and into a mock shed. A wooden frame was placed on top of the trailer that was taller than the barrels. If any part of the frame passed over the top of a barrel, points were deducted from your score. Also points were deducted for any inches the trailer was off center of the shed when you completed the course. Points were also deducted for each time you had to stop and pull forward to correct your direction. I could tell it was not going to be easy.

I had the opportunity to watch some of the other kids try to go through the course. Some finally gave up because they couldn't figure out how to get it done. Others made it through, but only with several errors. I was thankful I had practiced or I would have been one of the victims of the course.

When my turn came my dad reminded me to look where I wanted to go and make small adjustments to get there. He told me not to focus on the barrels. I made it through the first couple of barrels without any point deductions and began to gain confidence. I continued to follow my dad's advice and made it around all the barrels without a fault and headed for the shed. I kept an eye on the center of the shed and brought the trailer to a stop on dead center. Again I wasn't sure how I had done since I had not been watching all the barrels, but my smiling father told me I had not passed over a single barrel. He and others were also quite astonished. I was only 12 years old and those who were doing well were the 17 and 18 year old boys with considerably more experience. I was relieved and happy with my accomplishment. I did notice there was a great deal of discussion going on by the group of men doing the judging. My father was called over and the discussion continued.

When the contest was over it was announced that one of the 18 year old boys had won the competition. I don't remember being upset because I knew I had done the best I could do. It had been a fun experience for me. My dad had told me I had done a great job and I was looking forward to going home and reporting how well I had done to my mother, grandfather and uncle. On the way home my dad was quiet for awhile, then he told me he wanted me to know that in fact the judges had been unable to determine who the winner was. An 18 year old boy and I both had perfect scores. The determining factor was who was closest to the center of the shed and it was too close to call. He said the judges couldn't believe a 12 year old had done so well and were concerned I would be overwhelmed at the state competition, which was the next step for the winner. I realized then that was why the judges had called my dad over to their meeting. They apparently wanted his blessing on their decision and he chose wisely not to disagree with the judges.

While in reality this event had been a competition, I really hadn't looked at it that way at the time. I was not raised in a highly competitive environment. Farm life was built around cooperation not competition. We all had to chip in and help to accomplish the work that had to be done. Certainly we had some competitive events at school like track meets and softball games, but competition was not how I looked at life. I just wanted to do the best I could do. I knew my family would be proud of how well I had done and in my heart I knew I had done the best I could do.

When I entered the corporate world after college, I was astonished when I attended the national sales meeting of one of our clients. The theme for the meeting was "Beat the Competition". A speaker, who imitated General George Patton, was brought in to give an emotional speech about beating the competition. I kept thinking to myself, why aren't they talking about how they can better serve their customers? Why aren't they spending this time training the sales staff on how to do a better job of communicating the benefits and services the company has to offer? Why aren't they introducing new products and services that will help their customers more than their competition's products and services? Why aren't they practicing selling skills? This company did experience some short term growth, but eventually went bankrupt.

I don't want it to sound like I'm against competition. I believe strongly in the free enterprise system. In the long-term, I believe it brings the most good to the most people.

My point is that thinking just about beating someone else puts your mind in a negative state. It's a negative emotion and while it might give you some short-term pleasure when you beat someone, it will not give you long-term contentment. In fact, your life will be pretty stressful if beating others is your primary goal.

On the other hand, if your goal is to do the best you can, help as many people as possible with the best service and products available you will more than likely do better than your competition and win the race anyway. Plus your mind will be in a positive state and you will find a great deal more long-term happiness.

When I became a father and began experiencing the city life with my children I discovered sports were a dominant part of the picture. I discovered there were some wonderful parents who volunteered to coach the children and teach them the basics of the activity as well as how to compete and still be a good sport. I volunteered and thoroughly enjoyed the experience. While I knew nothing about soccer, it was the sport my children liked so I learned how to coach a team.

Competition can be a wonderful learning experience for children if the adults involved truly act like adults. Fortunately, most adults do. It teaches children team work, discipline, hard work, practice and digging deep to be the best they can be. Hopefully it also teaches them how to compete and still be a good sport. Hopefully it teaches them you don't have to hate your competition. You just want to do the best you can. If you perform better than your competition, the victory goes to you.

I believe the ritual of shaking hands after a game is a wonderful tradition. I see it as a thank you to the other competitor for testing you to see how good you can be.

Encourage your children to participate in organized sports, music, debate or other activities that provide competition. Help the children find an activity that fits their skills. They may not be a natural, however, perseverance and determination can be great equalizers and my experience is the children who have had to work the hardest are the ones who many times find the greatest success in future years.

"Industry, economy, honesty and kindness form a quartet of virtue that will never be improved upon."
James Olive

"You shouldn't charge for a broken bale." My farm experience

19. HONESTY

Since our farm was a dairy farm it was necessary for us to bale alfalfa in the summer months to feed the cattle in the winter. The hay would be harvested several times during the summer so my dad purchased a hay baler to accomplish the work. He was one of the few farmers in the area to own a baler, so he was hired by other farmers to bale their hay for them.

There were several jobs on the farm that were unpleasant, but this was one of the worst for my brother and me. Technology was not perfect in those days, so the mechanism that automatically tied the knots on the bales sometimes malfunctioned. When it did, there was an opportunity to stop the movement of the bales and hand tie the knot before the bale was expelled from the baler. Unfortunately, to know if the knot was tied properly by the machine, someone had to ride on the back of the baler and check each knot as it was tied. That job was assigned to my brother and me. It was a very unpleasant job with the dust and dry hay particles hanging in the air at the back of the baler. It was a job my brother and I both hated.

However, I did learn a lesson in honesty. The baler had an automatic counter that counted each bale as it was tied. At the end of the day you could look at the counter and determine how many bales had been made. Since my dad charged the other farmers by the bale it was an important number. The problem arose if a bale broke when it hit the ground and had to be baled again. This of course was recorded on the counter as another bale when in reality it was still just one bale. When a bale had to be redone, my dad would go to the counter and subtract the additional bale so the farmer wouldn't be charged for the redo of the bale.

I never really thought much about his action because honesty was a way of life in the farm community. I saw what he was doing as the honest, normal, right thing to do.

I believe the culture of honesty is deep in most farm communities. It comes from past generations needing to be able to trust each other to survive. A hand shake was all that was required to close a deal. I don't remember the subject of honesty being discussed very much in our family. It was such an understood, cultural rule that it didn't even need to be discussed.

I was to discover it wasn't quite so easy when we were raising our own children in the city. It wasn't an understood culture by some of the children in the city. Our children were exposed to situations I never faced as a child regarding decisions about honesty.

It came to my attention in a big way when I was complaining about loosing a small plastic tube needed to spray oil from a can of lubricant. I said I would need to buy another can of lubricant just to get the plastic tube. My young son stated I could just take the plastic tube from one of the cans in the store. I looked at him in disbelief and realized I had not done a very good job of teaching him about honesty. Even though my wife had made the children take back gum they had picked up at the grocery counter while she was checking out, he hadn't gotten the message from me. As I look back on it now I think it was such an understood value in my childhood I hadn't realized our children weren't growing up in the same community environment.

I took the opportunity to explain to him why taking it would be wrong. I happened to know the hardware store owner and I explained to our son that taking the plastic tube from his store would hurt him. I explained that I knew he worked very hard to take care of his customers and worked many hours to make a living at the store. I explained it would not be right to hurt him by stealing something from his store. I believe explaining it in human terms made sense to him. Prior to that I think the store was just some big impersonal place. Taking something from the store wouldn't seem to do any harm to anyone. Afterwards I wondered why I hadn't taken the time to explain this concept before. I believe I just assumed the children would understand it was wrong not to be honest. I realize now that in an environment that doesn't necessarily promote honesty on a day-to-day basis, the concept does need to be taught and explained to children on a regular basis.

Unfortunately some of our well known government officials, corporate executives and sports heroes haven't done a very good job of demonstrating honesty. That makes it even more critical that parents set a good example. It doesn't have to be one big example. It can be as simple as returning change to a clerk who has given you too much, or correcting a restaurant ticket if they forgot to charge you for something. When the children see you doing these acts of honesty it will communicate more to them than all the lectures you can give. And hopefully it will help them fight the temptation to do something dishonest that could cause them a great deal of trouble in the future.

Just as important as honesty keeping people out of trouble, honesty can also make them successful. As Mirabeau stated, "If honesty did not exist, we ought to invent it as the best means of getting rich."

People want to do business with those they trust, buy from people they trust, hire people they trust, work for people they trust, and be friends with people they trust.

Children need to be told that honesty is about more than just staying out of trouble. It's about leading a successful, happy life.

"Your built-in success mechanism must have a goal or target." Maxwell Maltz, "Psyco-Cybernetics"

"The ability to mentally visualize a desired future and take the necessary actions to reach that future is the first step toward achieving any kind of success." My most important lesson

20. CONCLUSION

There were many lessons I learned from being raised on a farm. Many I learned because I was blessed with parents who cared about me and knew the right things to do. As a child I didn't always think they were right and I'm sure they did make a mistake or two, as we all do as parents. Yet the life skills I needed to lead a successful life came from their guidance and the lessons learned from the farm environment.

If I were to identify the most important lesson I believe it would have to be "long-term thinking." In reviewing the stories I've related, it seems to be the common thread that runs through most of them.

If you analyze the people who are experiencing difficulty in life, whether it be financial, relationships, family, health, careers or the legal system, you'll often find it's because they made choices without thinking about the long-term consequences decisions would have on their life.

A study done by Walter Mischel at a preschool on the Stanford University campus supports this premise. Four-year-old children were given a marshmallow and told if they would wait to eat it until the person in charge returned from an errand they would be given two. If not, they would only be given one. Twelve to fourteen years later the children were located as adolescents. Those who could not think beyond the moment and ate the marshmallow were experiencing difficulties in their lives. Those who had already learned the ability to think beyond the moment, trust adults and had waited for the additional marshmallow were experiencing much greater success in life. The wonderful news is this ability can be "taught" to our children!

The farm environment was a wonderful place to learn this concept of long-term thinking. It was understood that you had to wait 8 months for the wheat crop to reach maturity. It was obvious you had to wait 3 years for a baby calf to grow old enough to begin producing milk. We had to wait for the potato plants to grow before they could be dug to provide new potatoes. Much of our life was centered around working and waiting.

I would like to think most farm children from my generation would have understood the concept of waiting for the second marshmallow. It would have only been natural for us to understand that patience was sometimes necessary.

Looking positively to the future, I believe, requires a combination of trust, faith and a positive attitude. Providing an environment where children can experience and learn these traits is, I believe, the most important job of parenting.

Using long-term thinking allows an individual to dream about the future they want and begin making decisions on a daily basis that will take them to their goals. It provides a framework for evaluating major decisions that have to be made. When multiple options are available, the one that will help reach the long-term goal is the one that should be chosen.

I hope the stories I've related to you have been enjoyable. I was blessed with good parents and a good environment. Hopefully the lessons I learned will be beneficial to you.